# A QUICK & EASY GUIDE TO
# ASEXUALITY

—— MOLLY MULDOON & WILL HERNANDEZ ——

# A QUICK & EASY GUIDE TO
# ASEXUALITY

—— MOLLY MULDOON & WILL HERNANDEZ ——

A LIMERENCE PRESS
PUBLICATION

# PUBLISHED BY LIMERENCE PRESS

LIMERENCE PRESS IS AN IMPRINT OF ONI-LION FORGE
PUBLISHING GROUP, LLC.

**JAMES LUCAS JONES,** president & publisher
**CHARLIE CHU,** e.v.p. of creative & business development
**STEVE ELLIS,** s.v.p. of games & operations
**ALEX SEGURA,** s.v.p. of marketing & sales
**MICHELLE NGUYEN,** associate publisher
**BRAD ROOKS,** director of operations
**AMBER O'NEILL,** special projects manager
**MARGOT WOOD,** director of marketing & sales
**KATIE SAINZ,** marketing manager
**HENRY BARAJAS,** sales manager
**TARA LEHMANN,** publicist
**HOLLY AITCHISON,** consumer marketing manager
**TROY LOOK,** director of design & production
**ANGIE KNOWLES,** production manager
**KATE Z. STONE,** senior graphic designer
**CAREY HALL,** graphic designer
**SARAH ROCKWELL,** graphic designer
**HILARY THOMPSON,** graphic designer
**VINCENT KUKUA,** digital prepress technician
**CHRIS CERASI,** managing editor
**JASMINE AMIRI,** senior editor
**SHAWNA GORE,** senior editor
**AMANDA MEADOWS,** senior editor
**ROBERT MEYERS,** senior editor, licensing
**DESIREE RODRIGUEZ,** editor
**GRACE SCHEIPETER,** editor
**ZACK SOTO,** editor
**BEN EISNER,** game developer
**JUNG LEE,** logistics coordinator
**KUIAN KELLUM,** warehouse assistant

**JOE NOZEMACK,** publisher emeritus

Written by
**MOLLY MULDOON**
Drawn and co-written by
**WILL HERNANDEZ**
Lettering by
**ANGIE KNOWLES**
Cover illustration by
**WILL HERNANDEZ**

Designed by
**KATE Z. STONE**
Edited by
**ARI YARWOOD**
& **AMANDA MEADOWS**

**LimerencePress.com**
🐦 limerencepress
🐦 📷 f onipress

**passingfair.com**
📷 🐦 passingfair

**willhernandezdraws.com**
🐦 willhdraws

**First Edition: March 2022**
ISBN 978-1-62010-859-8
eISBN 978-1-62010-860-4

**Library of Congress Control Number: 2020939102**

Hey, folks!
Welcome to
A Quick & Easy Guide
to Asexuality!

Just got a
few things to note
before we get
started...

## Who Should Read This?

Anyone! This is an extremely basic introduction to
asexuality for asexual people, folks questioning whether
they might be ace, and anyone hoping to understand
more about asexuality from two rad aces
(which would be us, hi again!).

## Content Warning!

Some things we (briefly) cover might be triggering
or upsetting. Unfortunately, our society is imperfect,
and our lives reflect this. We'll discuss harmful stereotypes
and tropes that run rampant in pop culture and society at
large. There will be mentions of sexual violence, medical
discrimination, depression, rejection and invalidation, and
general internet nastiness. Nothing will be graphically
depicted or discussed to a graphic degree,
but please proceed with caution.

## What We're Covering:

This book will cover what asexuality is, how it affects
different aspects of a person's life, and how it is viewed
by culture and society. We'll also discuss common
misconceptions, dating and sex, representation—
or the lack thereof—and our own personal
thoughts and experiences with all of this.

## What We're NOT Covering:

This is a quick and easy guide, so we focused on the topics above.
If you are looking for specific sexual instruction, relationship advice,
or deeper analysis of the "Split Attraction Model," we have listed resources in
the back of the book that might help! Ultimately, this is a positive exploration of a
sexuality that isn't widely understood by society—because everyone deserves
to be accepted and respected. We hope that you learn something from this and
maybe even do some of your own exploring after you read!
Either way, we're glad you're with us.

# What is Asexuality?

11

# Common Questions Aces Get Asked:

14

SHADES OF GRAY

# The
# Spectrum of
# Asexuality

Remember that spectrum we were talking about? It has to do with that.

A lot of people assume asexual people are utterly sex-repulsed and want nothing to do with it. Those people are to one **far side** of the spectrum.

Most people don't fall so easily in those categories, though, and they are somewhere along this spectrum from **sex-repulsed** to super **sex-charmed**.

That's why so many ace people identify as...

GRAY-A!

Even though most people will just call themselves ace, a lot of people are more in a **gray area**, hence **gray-a**. Ace is just an easier shorthand.

Like saying you're from Boston or Seattle rather than your suburb when you're far from home. Makes it easier for people.

21

In my case, I identify as **demisexual**, a type of gray-a.

Demisexual means you can feel attracted to people but only after you've formed an emotional bond with them, be it friendship, a romantic relationship, or something else.

To be honest, I only heard about demisexuality for the first time from reading fan-fiction. It was like a light bulb went off.

It explained why I could acknowledge that an actor was good-looking but not understand the girls fawning over him...

...while still feeling the pitter-patter of my heart when my high school crush walked by.

As for myself, though I use "asexual" as a pretty accurate and **baseline descriptor** to generally sum up my experience. I feel my identity is a bit more complicated than any set of labels can describe...

On the one hand, I can comfortably say that I've never felt any real "sexual attraction" to anybody I can recall...

I've never been able to look at someone as other than their mind and personality, no matter the situation...

That's not to say I can't acknowledge when someone has that "sex appeal" going for 'em, but my brain just kinda goes, "Yeah, I don't care, that's still a regular human thing."

And, hehe, funnily enough, I feel I've made many sex worker friends over the years due to the fact my brain just doesn't respond to the "would-be adverts" in the typical way.

But on the other hand, I'm not repulsed by it either. In fact, I think it's really cool and fun and interesting to think about!

It's really facinating anthropologically to see and learn about how much of a driver sex is worldwide, and how it impacts and plays a role in every nation and culture.

And back to a personal level, I'm still very open to the possibility of sex in my own relationships, though I won't die if that isn't a possibility for any reason, since it's not much of a requirement I hold.

I, and many other aces, in fact, do have a perfectly functioning sex drive. But for me, it bubbles up from inside rather than being "activated" externally.

So not being directed at anyone in particular, I'm fine managing myself, with or without company.

I could go into more nuance than can fit in a single book. Heck, I haven't even **begun** to talk about my feelings on romance and relationship stuff!

TLDR:
The spectrum is complicated, and humans are more complicated than a series of binaries.

25

# Asexuality
# and
# Aromanticism

While aromantics are not necessarily asexual and asexuals aren't necessarily aromantic...

Sexual

Aroaces!

Romance

...some people don't really feel romantic or sexual attraction for anyone. Those people are **aromantic asexuals**, or **aroaces**.

Of course, we've talked about areas of gray before, so most people won't be 100 percent on either axis.

But understanding the difference between **romantic** and **sexual attraction** has helped many ace and aro people understand themselves and realize other people feel the same way, too!

30

31

# Dating
# While
# Asexual

As of the writing of this book, there is just one dating app for ace people, and it's...not great. There are some websites that let you list your sexuality as ace or demi, but people don't tend to read that.

Also, for people that are more in the gray area, being with someone who is more sex-repulsed than them or more sex-enthused than them could pose a problem.

Meanwhile, say you're demisexual and you're on a date with a nice person. It's pretty hard to tell them, "Well, I like you as a person, but I'm not sexually attracted to you right now. Those feelings may come in the future, after we form a deeper emotional bond, but I can't promise that will happen, either."

That's a lot to put on anyone.

34

It can also mean we are very bad at flirting or picking up signals from other people.

I always call the way I flirt "Jane Benneting," after the oldest sister in *Pride and Prejudice*. She's so nice to everyone that no one knows she's partial to Mr. Bingley.

Or, as it usually goes with me: "Why can't you see that when I'm nice to everyone I'm being polite, but when I'm being nice to you, it's because I like you?"

Very clear, I know.

And myself, as shy as I might get, I'm actually pretty flirtatious by nature, even with friends. So there's a bit of disconnect between doing it because I want someone's attention and just being comfortable around a person. As a result, I end up confusing myself as to how I'm feeling.

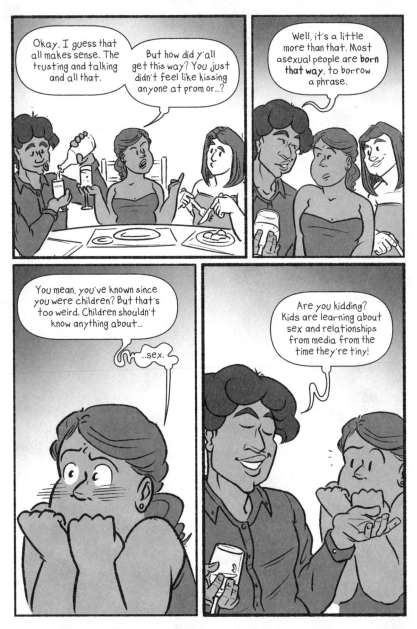

37

# Growing
# Up
# Ace

40

41

To an extent, it left me feeling very isolated and different from everyone else I'd come to encounter by then.

Like, there were feelings I'd never experience and it made me "broken."

For a good chunk of my life, I ended up self-isolating out of not knowing enough about myself and feeling I just wasn't meant to fit in...

...it led to a series of other mental health issues: depression, social anxiety disorder, PTSD...

...all of which I still have to struggle with as an adult, heh.

45

# Ace
# Stereotypes

THE ASEXUAL GENIUS TROPE

This is almost always men.

When it comes to stereotypes for women, it tends to be one of two things. You're either a victim of trauma...

...or you're a "prude."

The trauma narrative implies that the only reason women wouldn't want to have sex is because they'd been hurt in the past.

Which we know isn't true, because a lot of asexual people have felt this way their whole life but didn't know what they were feeling was normal.

While many, many people are victims of sexual assault or trauma, this won't make a person asexual.

It might make them form a set of trauma responses, which can include sex-repulsion, but it won't change their fundamental selves.

You are not what is done to you, and this is a dangerous narrative to present.

Likewise, the "prude" narrative is all wrapped around the misconception that asexual people are no fun, repressed, or keeping a part of themselves locked away out of some desire to "be better" than other people, kind of like the asexual genius trope.

These people would be "way more fun if they just let down their hair a little," then maybe people would like them.

The problem, of course, is this implies the person actually does feel sexual attraction but is repressing for "moral" reasons. The "prude" is seen as rejecting a part of their humanity, and the world says the prude will be more authentic and more likable if they "let go."

This is clearly a problem, because it, again, makes asexuality an abnormality. Asexual people are just people who don't feel sexual attraction. They are in no way judging others for their choices. They're just **living their life.**

# The "A" in
# LGBTQIA+

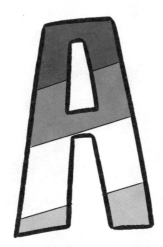

Artist's Note: Collected from real online comments. I don't wanna do that again...

Finding an **ace community** to join and chat with other ace people is probably the best thing you can do when you're just figuring yourself out, or pretty much any time after that.

Talking with other ace people has been the most affirming part of understanding my demisexuality, and it helps that most people are super kind and chill.

No one understands better than other people who have been through the same thing.

And being able to interact with new people, make like-minded friends, and learn more online has helped me develop more confidence and value in myself despite my offline limitations.

Plus, it doesn't hurt that asexuality's two unofficial mascots are **axolotls** and **cake**.

The cutest thing and the most delicious thing.

Taking that into account, you'll want to figure out if you want to **"come out"** or not.

You don't have to tell people you're asexual if you don't want to, as it's no one's business but your own. But, you also have **nothing** to be embarrassed about.

I didn't tell anyone until I started writing this book, since it'd be public knowledge soon, anyway.

I'm super happy with the friends I've made and the chance to be an example for other aces to show that you can happily be yourself.

But it was also a weird conversation with my mom that we haven't really talked about since.

Oof, I feel that!

I'm not "out" to anyone outside of my online friend groups currently. Though, that may change with this book.

And, although it doesn't impact my day-to-day life too much, I tend to get nervous about how my "traditional" family will take it.

65

All you allos! If your friend, family member, coworker, or anyone comes out to you as being asexual, the best way to support them is to just **listen** to what they have to say and be **understanding**.

There's a good chance your friend is still figuring things out, and just being there for them is extremely helpful.

The important thing is not to try and "fix" them. It's not something to be fixed and will only make your friend feel **uncomfortable**.

Deep down, you know your friend. They haven't changed. Just treat them like you **care** about them and you're on the right track.

# Resources

## Books on Asexuality

**Ace: What Asexuality Reveals About Desire, Society, and the Meaning of Sex**
by Angela Chen, Beacon Press, September 2020

**Asexuality: A Brief Introduction** (free PDF)
AsexualityArchive.com,
http://www.asexualityarchive.com/wp-content/
uploads/2012/05/AsexualityABriefIntroduction.pdf

**A Quick & Easy Guide to Queer and Trans Identities**
by Mady G. and J.R. Zuckerberg, Limerence Press, 2019

**The Invisible Orientation: An Introduction to Asexuality**
by Julie Sondra Decke, Skyhorse Publishing, September 2014

## Websites - Education, Resources, and Forums

**Asexuality.org**
https://www.asexuality.org/

**The Trevor Project**
https://www.thetrevorproject.org/
trvr_support_center/asexual/

**Queer As Cat, POC resources**
https://queerascat.tumblr.com/apoc-resources

**List of Ace-Friendly Therapists, Fuck Yeah Asexual**
https://fuckyeahasexual.tumblr.com/post/150192839768/
ace-friendly-therapists-masterpost-build

# Will Hernandez

is a lifelong artist, and a first-time published comic creator/co-author. Though a passionate storyteller and draftsman, Will is also on an endless journey of discovery, looking to learn more about the world and, in turn, themself. Through ups and downs, they've discovered themself to be on the asexual spectrum, growing ever more curious of the role sexuality and gender play in society, and fond of the culture it creates.

# Molly Muldoon

is a former scholar and bookseller, current librarian and writer, and always demisexual fan fiction enthusiast. Her works include *The Cardboard Kingdom, Dead Weight: Murder at Camp Bloom,*

and the forthcoming *The Cardboard Kingdom: Roar of the Beast*. Although she's spent the past ten years globetrotting, she currently lives in Portland, Oregon, with her ridiculous cat, Jamie McKitten.